MW01131067

The 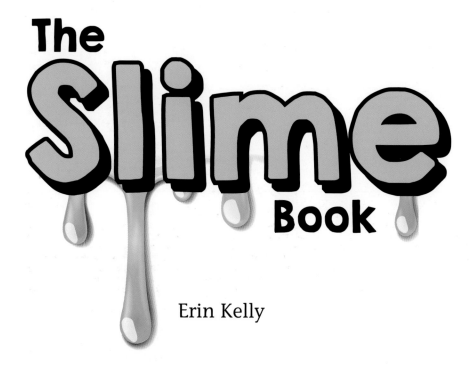 Book

Erin Kelly

Brought to you by the editors of

Let's Find Out
My Weekly Reader

Children's Press®
An imprint of Scholastic Inc.

How to Read This Book

This book is for kids and grown-ups to read together—side by side!

A 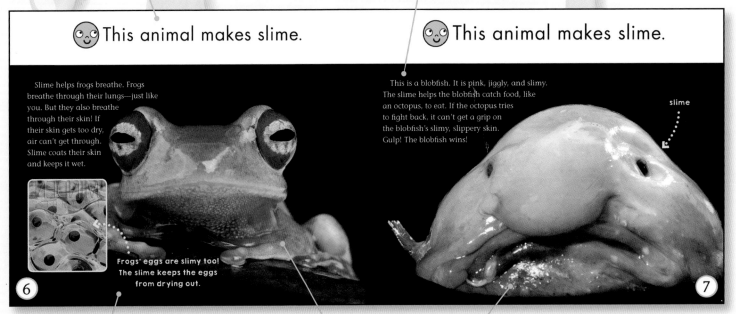 means it is the kid's turn to read.

A grown-up can read the rest.

Simple text for kids who are learning to read

Harder text—that builds knowledge and vocabulary— for grown-ups to read aloud

This animal makes slime.

This animal makes slime.

Slime helps frogs breathe. Frogs breathe through their lungs—just like you. But they also breathe through their skin! If their skin gets too dry, air can't get through. Slime coats their skin and keeps it wet.

Frogs' eggs are slimy too! The slime keeps the eggs from drying out.

This is a blobfish. It is pink, jiggly, and slimy. The slime helps the blobfish catch food, like an octopus, to eat. If the octopus tries to fight back, it can't get a grip on the blobfish's slimy, slippery skin. Gulp! The blobfish wins!

slime

6

7

Nonfiction text features like charts and captions

Bright photos to talk about

2

Table of Contents

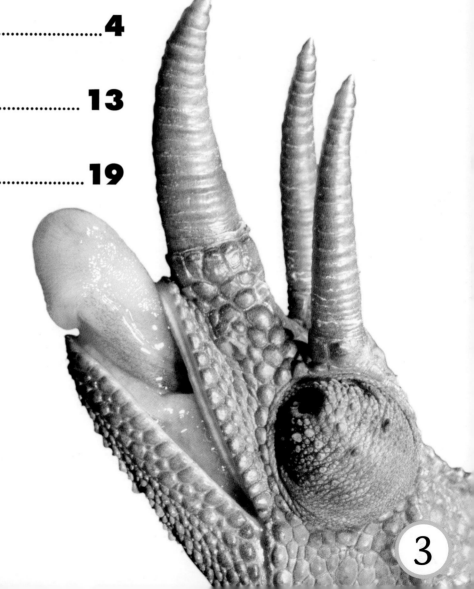

3

4

Chapter 1

Animals Make Slime

A lot of animals make slime. It may look gross, but it helps them!

Frogs and their eggs are covered in slime.

This animal makes slime.

Slime helps frogs breathe. Frogs breathe through their lungs—just like you. But they also breathe through their skin! If their skin gets too dry, air can't get through. Slime coats their skin and keeps it wet.

The slime that covers frog eggs keeps them from drying out.

This animal makes slime.

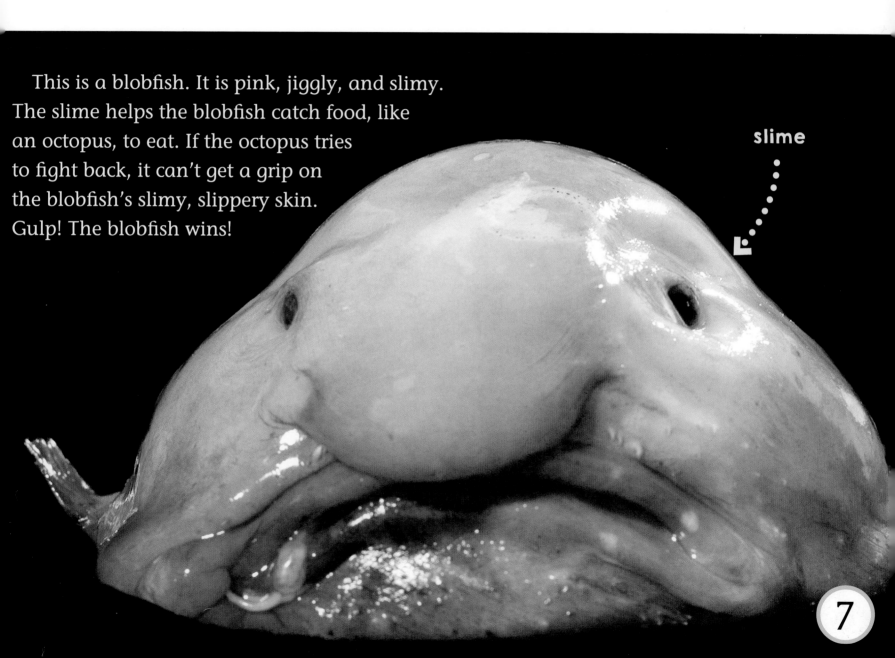

This is a blobfish. It is pink, jiggly, and slimy. The slime helps the blobfish catch food, like an octopus, to eat. If the octopus tries to fight back, it can't get a grip on the blobfish's slimy, slippery skin. Gulp! The blobfish wins!

slime

This animal makes slime.

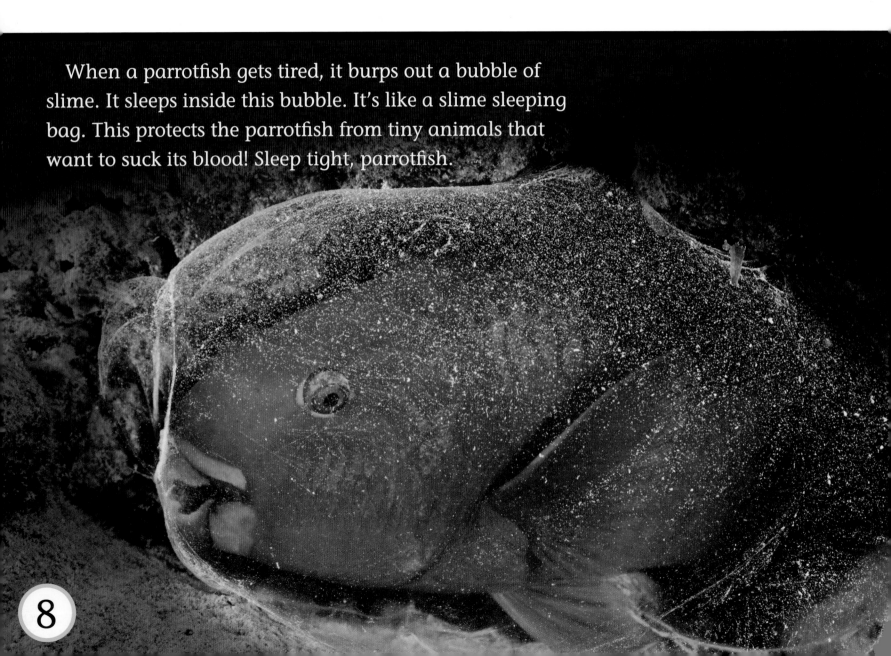

When a parrotfish gets tired, it burps out a bubble of slime. It sleeps inside this bubble. It's like a slime sleeping bag. This protects the parrotfish from tiny animals that want to suck its blood! Sleep tight, parrotfish.

This animal makes slime.

Hagfish are also known as slime **eels**. They swim along the bottom of the ocean, eating dead fish. When a **predator** comes along, watch out! The hagfish squirts a mouthful of choking slime.

Scientists are trying to figure out the secret to hagfish slime's stickiness.

This animal makes slime.

A giraffe's long tongue is covered with slime. This slimy **saliva** comes in handy when giraffes eat leaves from the thorny acacia [uh-KAY-shuh] tree.

thorn

The slime coats the thorns. This lets the thorns pass through the giraffe's body without hurting it.

 # This animal makes slime.

Slime helps chameleons grab lunch. When a chameleon sticks out its slimy tongue to nab an insect, that insect gets stuck tight. Gulp!

What Chameleons Eat

| crickets | cockroaches | mealworms |

This animal makes slime.

And its slime has **venom**! When a Komodo dragon bites into its prey, venomous slime shoots from holes between its teeth. The prey is paralyzed—it can't move.

This giant lizard does not live in the United States.

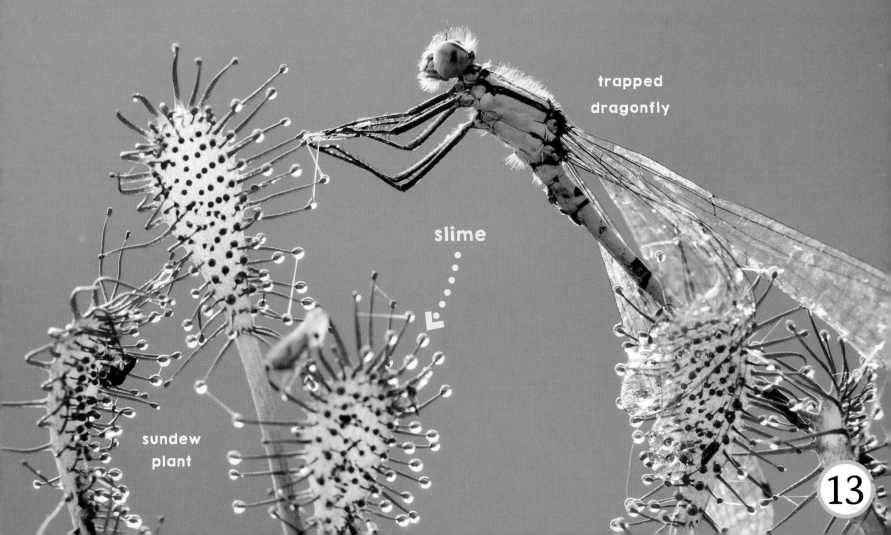

Chapter 2

Plants Make Slime

Plants make slime that helps them—and us!

trapped
dragonfly

slime

sundew
plant

This plant makes slime.

Slime covers the sundew's pretty red **tentacles**. It looks like **nectar**. When insects land on the plant, they get stuck! The leaves then curl around the insect. Goodbye, insect. You've just become dinner.

This plant makes slime.

Pitcher plants have leaves shaped like cups—and these cups are filled with sweet, sticky slime. Insects smell the slime. They think it's yummy nectar.

When an insect tries to drink, it gets stuck. The slime then dissolves the insect into plant food.

☺ This plant makes slime.

Have you ever cut open a pumpkin? Pumpkins are filled with slimy **pulp** and seeds. The slime makes the seeds stick to your hands!

These plants make slime.

When fruits and vegetables get old, they start to rot. Mold grows. They get slimy and gross! Time to toss them into the **compost bin**.

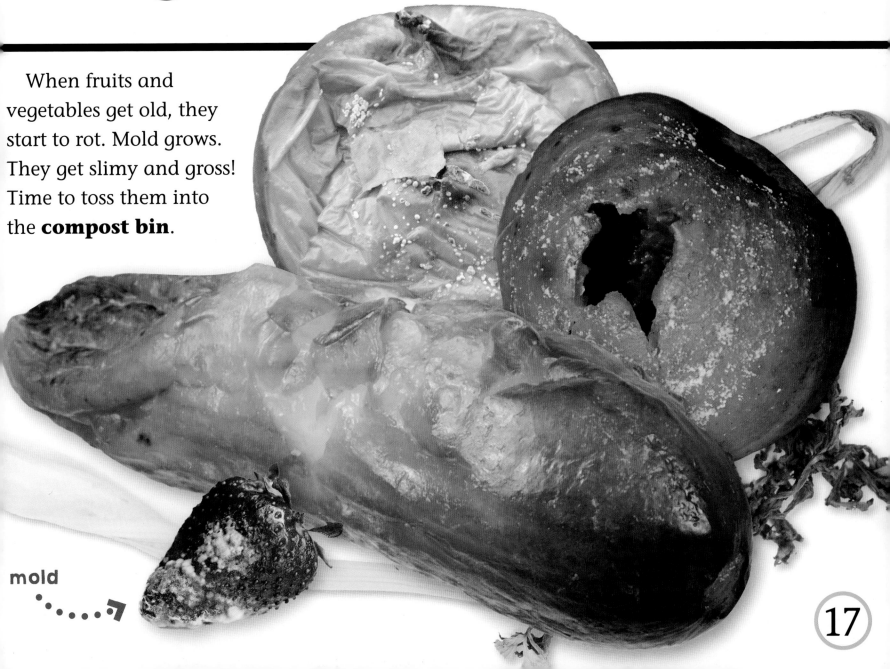

mold
•••••⌐

This plant makes slime.

When you break open an aloe leaf, it oozes clear slime. The aloe plant's slime protects it. When an insect bites the leaf, it chokes on the slime. That teaches the insect to stay away!

Some people use aloe to soothe sunburns.

18

Chapter 3
We Make Slime

We make slime. It keeps us healthy. But don't share your slime!

19

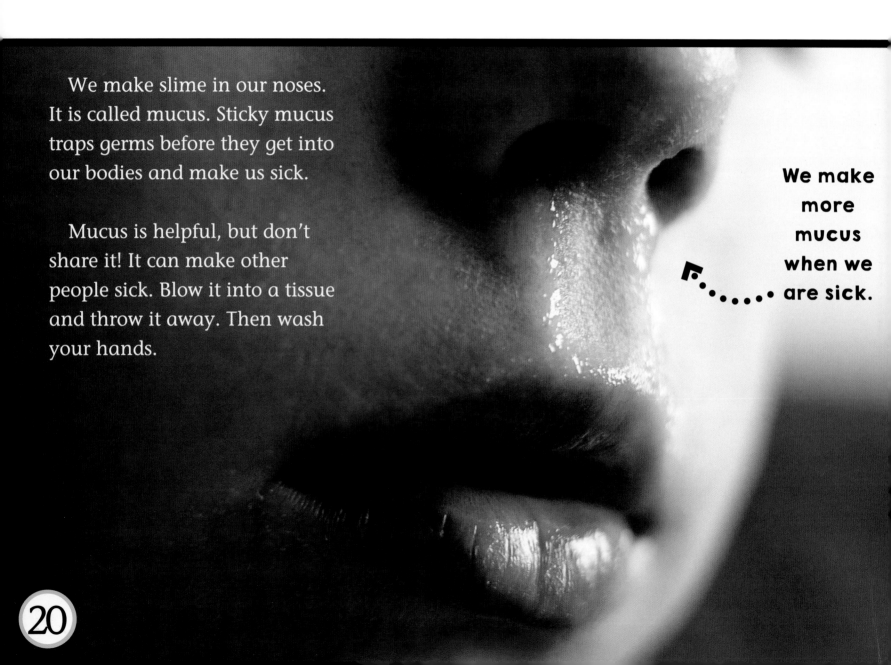We make slime.

We make slime in our noses. It is called mucus. Sticky mucus traps germs before they get into our bodies and make us sick.

Mucus is helpful, but don't share it! It can make other people sick. Blow it into a tissue and throw it away. Then wash your hands.

We make more mucus when we are sick.

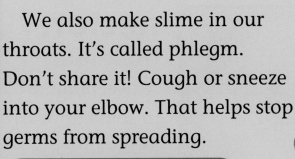 We make slime.

We also make slime in our throats. It's called phlegm. Don't share it! Cough or sneeze into your elbow. That helps stop germs from spreading.

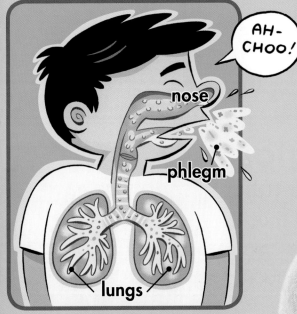

AH-CHOO!

nose

phlegm

lungs

At night, mucus and phlegm can drip into our lungs and make us cough.

Slime is everywhere! It may be gross, but it sure is helpful.

21

Glossary

compost bin:
(**kom**-pohst bin)
A container that holds a
mixture of rotted leaves
and food that will be
added to the soil
to make it richer

nectar:
(**nek**-tuhr)
A sweet liquid
in some flowers.
Many insects
drink nectar.

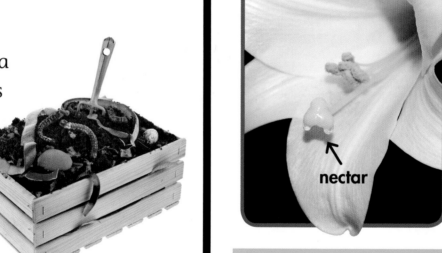

nectar

eels: (eelz)
Long, snakelike fish. Hagfish look like eels,
but they are not.

predator:
(**pred**-uh-tuhr)
An animal that
hunts other
animals for food

pulp:
(puhlp)

The soft, squishy insides of fruits and vegetables. This pumpkin pulp has seeds in it.

tentacles:
(**ten**-tuh-kuhlz)

Long, thin, flexible parts that some animals and plants have

saliva: (suh-**ly**-vuh)

The clear liquid in your mouth, or in an animal's mouth. Saliva keeps the mouth wet and helps animals and people swallow their food.

venom:
(**ven**-uhm)

Poison made by some animals. It can hurt or kill.

Index

Photographs ©: cover main: Torsten Blackwood/AFP/Getty Images; cover smiley faces and throughout: Giuseppe_R/Shutterstock; back cover chameleon: Otto Hahn/Picture Press/Getty Images; back cover background: Gromovataya/Shutterstock; 2: TAW4/Shutterstock; 3: Kim Taylor/Minden Pictures; 4-5: Pete Oxford; 6 main: Matthijs Kuijpers/Minden Pictures; 6 inset: Jan van der Greef/Minden Pictures; 7: Kerryn Parkinson/ZUMAPRESS/Newscom; 8: R. Dirscherl/Blickwinkel/age fotostock; 9 main: Brandon Cole Marine Photography/Alamy Images; 9 inset hand: PJF Military Collection/Alamy Images; 9 inset hagfish: Elizabeth Beard/Moment/Getty Images; 10 left: Andy Rouse/Minden Pictures; 10 right: Sam Scott-Hunter/Dorling Kindersley/Getty Images; 10 background: Robert Adrian Hillman/Shutterstock; 11 inset left: tea maeklong/Shutterstock; 11 inset center: 7th Son Studio/Shutterstock; 11 inset right: Bezzangi/Shutterstock; 11 background: Otto Hahn/Picture Press/Getty Images; 12: Dave Fleetham/Design Pics/Getty Images; 13: Willi Rolfes/ullstein bild/Getty Images; 14 bottom left: Jean-Michel Lenoir/Minden Pictures; 14 main: Andy Sands/Minden Pictures; 15 main: kunmom/Shutterstock; 15 inset: Michael Durham/Minden Pictures; 16: Fortunato Photography; 17 center: sunstock/iStockphoto; 17 top left: agrofruti/Shutterstock; 17 bottom left: rsooll/Shutterstock; 17 bottom right: Aku Alip/Shutterstock; 18 right pot: Hurst Photo/Shutterstock; 18 right plant: Lev Kropotov/Shutterstock; 18 left: Hekla/Shutterstock; 19 left: Oksana Kuzmina/Shutterstock; 19 right: real444/iStockphoto; 20: mrs/Moment/Getty Images; 21 inset: Kelly Kennedy; 21 main: Fortunato Photography; 22 top left: Madlen/Shutterstock; 22 top right: Yevettem/Dreamstime; 22 bottom left: Sakdinon Kadchiangsaen/Shutterstock; 22 bottom right: kyslynskahal/Shutterstock; 23 top left: Barry L. Runk/Grant Heilman Photography/Alamy Images; 23 bottom left: Dan Kosmayer/Shutterstock; 23 top right: Laurie Campbell/Minden Pictures; 23 bottom right snake: reptiles4all/Shutterstock; 23 bottom right inset: Joe McDonald/Shutterstock.

Library of Congress Cataloging-in-Publication Data

Names: Kelly, Erin Suzanne, 1965- author.
Title: The slime book / by Erin Kelly.
Description: New York, NY : Children's Press, an imprint of Scholastic Inc., 2019. | Series: Side by side | Includes index.
Identifiers: LCCN 2018029944| ISBN 9780531131114 (library binding) | ISBN 9780531136492 (paperback)
Subjects: LCSH: Secretion--Juvenile literature. | Body fluids--Juvenile literature. | Mucus--Juvenile literature.
Classification: LCC QP190 .K45 2019 | DDC 612.4--dc23

Brought to you by the editors of Let's Find Out®. Original Design by Sandy Mayer, Joan Michael and Judith E. Christ for Scholastic Inc.